NEWTON IN 90 MINUTES

In the same series by the same authors:

John and Mary Gribbin

NEWTON
(1642–1727)
in 90 minutes

Constable · London

First published in Great Britain 1997
by Constable and Company Limited
3 The Lanchesters, 162 Fulham Palace Road
London W6 9ER
Copyright © John and Mary Gribbin 1997
The right of John and Mary Gribbin to be identified
as authors of this work has been asserted by them
in accordance with the Copyright,
Designs and Patents Act 1988
ISBN 0 09 477040 9
Set in Linotype Sabon by
Rowland Phototypesetting Ltd,
Bury St Edmunds, Suffolk
Printed in Great Britain by
St Edmundsbury Press Ltd,
Bury St Edmunds, Suffolk

A CIP catalogue record for this book
is available from the British Library

Contents

Newton in context

Isaac Newton was the greatest scientist of all time. Although the first steps had been taken by Galileo Galilei, it was Newton who perfected the modern technique of scientific investigation in which ideas are tested and refined by comparison with experiment, instead of being plucked out of the air as more or less inspired speculations. Although Newton's direct discoveries and inventions in science were outstanding – he discovered the law of gravity and the laws of motion, made important advances in the understanding of light, designed and built with his own hands a new kind of telescope *and* invented the mathematical technique of calculus – it was his way of doing science that both made all this possible and transformed the investigation of the natural world.

Newton was quite clear about the importance of his approach to science, and how it differed from the approach taken by most of his contemporaries. He once wrote that:

The best and safest way of philosophizing seems to be, first to enquire diligently into the properties of things, and to establish those properties by experiments and then to proceed slowly to hypotheses for the explanation of them. For hypotheses should be employed only in explaining the properties of things, but not assumed in determining them; unless so far as they may furnish experiments.

This is at the heart of modern science. If your favourite idea about the nature of the world does not match up with the results of experiment, then it is wrong.

This is so deeply ingrained in anyone who has studied science that it is hard to appreciate just what a big step forward it was in the seventeenth century. But in Newton's day, there were still people who would argue, when he put forward his ideas about light, that these ideas were so obviously wrong, there was no need to carry out experiments to test them!

Largely thanks to his scientific approach to problems, and to his towering intellect, Newton removed the need to invoke magic or the supernatural to explain the workings of the Universe. Although Nicholas Copernicus had suggested that the Earth moved around the Sun, and Galileo had gathered a wealth of evidence that it did so, before Newton nobody knew what held the planets in their orbits, or what kept the stars in their places in the sky. It was Newton who showed that the Universe works in accordance with precise rules, or laws. The motions the planets, comets and, by implication, even the stars could be explained by the same laws that applied to the fall of an apple or the flight of a cannonball here on Earth. His law of gravitation and laws of motion are *universal* laws that apply everywhere, and at all times.

Galileo was born in 1564 and died in 1642. Newton was born within twelve months of the death of Galileo, and died in 1727. Their lives were overlapped by René Descartes (1596–1650), who, as we shall see, passed on an improved version of Galileo's ideas about inertia to Newton, giving him a key ingredient in formulating his laws of motion.

In 1564 the world was a mysterious place. What passed for science was the ancient lore of Aristotle – purely 'philosophical' ideas, unsullied by any contact with something as basic as an experiment, and enshrined by centuries of tradition – and any ideas about the Universe at large were mainly superstitious nonsense. In 1727, the modern image of the Universe as a great machine, ticking away as steadily and as predictably as clockwork, was firmly established (at least for the educated and literate members of society). In a sense, the Universe had been tamed.

But don't picture this clockwork image as a modern wristwatch, unobtrusively marking the passage of time. Picture instead a great cathedral clock of the early eighteenth century, driven by the swing of a huge pendulum (itself following laws first worked out by Galileo), with many interconnecting cogs and gearwheels, working together not only to mark the passage of time but to drive a complicated mechanism controlling the motion of elaborate tableaux including moving figures of the saints, and striking a variety of bells at appointed hours and quarters.

Newton's work made it clear that, like the complexity of those clocks, driven by a simple swinging pendulum, the Universe obeys simple laws which are intelligible to the human mind. It is these simple laws that interact to produce the complexity of the world we see around us. And that realization, plus the experimental method, is the underpinning of all of modern science.

Life and work

Isaac Newton came from a line of successful, upwardly mobile farmers, who had no tradition of learning whatsoever – neither his father nor his paternal grandfather could read or even write their own name. The grandfather, Robert Newton, was born around 1570, and as well as inheriting land at Woolsthorpe in Lincolnshire he prospered sufficiently to add to his property by purchasing the manor of Woolsthorpe in 1623. With it came the improved social status of Lord of the Manor of Woolsthorpe. This social elevation was probably an important factor in enabling Robert's oldest surviving son, Isaac, to become betrothed to Hannah Ayscough in 1639.

The Ayscoughs were the social superiors of the Newtons (Hannah's father, James, was described as a 'gentleman' in official documents), and brought to the prospective marriage property worth £50 a year. Robert made Isaac the heir to his entire Woolsthorpe property, including the Lordship of the Manor.

Far from being illiterate, the Ayscoughs were well educated. Hannah's brother

William was a Cambridge graduate and clergyman who took up a good living at a nearby village, Burton Coggles, in 1642. That was the year in which Hannah and Isaac Newton married, in April, some six months after the death of Robert Newton. In another six months Isaac himself also died, leaving his widow comfortably provided for but pregnant with a baby that was born, prematurely, on Christmas Day, and christened Isaac in memory of its father.

At least, it was Christmas Day in England. The Gregorian calendar had been introduced in Catholic countries in 1582, but in Britain suspicion of Popish trickery prevented the reform from being applied until 1752. At the time 'our' Isaac Newton was born, the Continental calendar was ten days ahead, and it was already 4 January. That is why it is really cheating to say that Newton was born in the same year in which Galileo died (on 8 January 1642 according to the Gregorian calendar); the 'coincidence' depends on using dates from two different calendar systems.

Another calendrical complication arises from the fact that in England at that time the legal date for New Year's Day was 25 March.

This is still enshrined in the UK Tax Year, which now begins in early April (thanks to the Gregorian calendar reform). We shall ignore this complication and give dates as if the year began on 1 January, in line with modern practice.

Whatever the date, when Isaac was born he was so small that, as he used to recount fondly in later life, he could have been fitted into a quart pot (it is not clear whether he ever *was* treated that way), and he was not expected to live. But he survived and flourished until he was three years old, when his life was turned upside-down.

Many other lives were being turned upside-down around that time, by the English Civil War, which ran from 1642 to 1648 and led to the beheading of Charles I and the establishment of the Commonwealth in 1649. Although the repercussions of these upheavals would affect Newton in later life, the turmoil of the Civil War itself seems to have largely passed Woolsthorpe by. Newton's upheaval in 1645 was much more personal – his mother remarried, and he was sent to live with his maternal grandparents.

Hannah's second marriage was a business-

like affair. Barnabas Smith, her new husband, was a wealthy 63-year-old who had buried his first wife in June 1644. He was the Rector of North Witham, less than 3 kilometres from Woolsthorpe, and had looked around for a suitable replacement, settling on Mrs Hannah Newton and approaching her through an intermediary. On the advice of her brother, Hannah accepted, on condition that her new husband immediately settled a piece of land on young Isaac; she went off to live with Barnabas Smith in the rectory, where she bore him two daughters and a son before he died at the age of 71 in 1653. Hannah, her wealth considerably enhanced by the inheritance from her second husband, then moved back to Woolsthorpe, and reclaimed Isaac for her own household. But for eight crucial years the boy had been living as a solitary child with his elderly grandparents.

This is usually presented as an entirely bad experience for Isaac, and it is hardly likely that he enjoyed those years. His relationship with his grandfather (the 'gentleman') was such that he never once mentioned him in his writings, and Isaac himself was not mentioned in the grandfather's will. But although he was lonely and probably unloved (a list of 'sins' which he wrote down a few years later includes 'threatening my father and mother Smith to burn them and the house over them'), the Ayscough experience provided him with one thing that he might not otherwise have had – an education.

There is no reason to think that Isaac Newton senior, had he lived, would have thought it worth having his son, destined to be a farmer, educated at all. It might have occurred to Hannah, had she stayed a lonely widow – but, equally likely, she might have wanted the boy to learn about the farm as soon as possible. To the elder Ayscoughs, though, it was natural to send the boy to day school, and set him on the road to a better education than a farmer's son might expect. Besides, school kept him out of the house.

Isaac returned to his mother's home in 1653, but less than two years later, when he was 12, he was sent away to study at the Grammar School in Grantham, some 8 kilometres away, where he lodged with the family of an apothecary, Mr Clark. The school was a good one and provided a grounding in the

Classics – mainly Latin, with some Greek – and a little mathematics. It taught nothing else, but the Latin would prove invaluable to Newton in his scientific career, because it was then still the universal language used for communication by academics across Europe, and in which important books were written.

The school itself had a notable old boy, the poet and philosopher Henry More (1614–87), who by 1654 was a Senior Fellow of Christ's College, Cambridge. The Clarks were no ordinary apothecary's family, for Mrs Clark had a brother, Humphrey Babington, who was a Fellow of Trinity College, but spent most of his time at Boothby Pagnell, near Grantham, where he was rector. So there were people in young Isaac's circle of acquaintances in Grantham who could recognize talent when they saw it, and were in a position to help it progress.

Isaac seems to have been as lonely at school as he had been with his grandparents. He enjoyed the company of girls more than boys, and one of them later recollected that he was a 'sober, silent, thinking lad'. He did get into one famous fight with a bigger boy, rousing himself to such a passion that he gave the larger lad a thorough thrashing, and so established a reputation which prevented him from being bullied. But his greatest delights were solitary study and manufacturing mechanical devices, including a working model of a windmill. He also caused one of the earliest recorded UFO scares by flying a kite at night with a paper lantern attached to it, thereby causing 'not a little discourse on market days, among the country people, when over their mugs of ale'. To his schoolboy companions, he must have seemed too clever by half, and was never liked.

At the end of 1659, when Newton was approaching the age of 17, he left the school to learn how to manage the land he would one day inherit from his mother. He was absolutely hopeless as a farmer, neglecting his work in order to read books, and being fined on several occasions for allowing animals in his care to wander and damage other farmers' crops. One anecdote records that on the way from Grantham to Woolsthorpe there is a steep hill, where it was usual to dismount and lead one's horse to the top before remounting. The story goes that Isaac arrived home with a book in one hand and the bridle in the other, his horse trailing along behind him, as he had forgotten to remount.

While Isaac was making a mess of farming, Hannah's brother William had been urging her to let the boy go to university. The school-master in Grantham, Henry Stokes, was so eager not to lose his star pupil that he offered to take him into his own home, without being paid for lodgings, if she would let him return to Grantham. Eventually, she agreed. In the autumn of 1660 (the year of the Restoration of the monarchy in England) Isaac went back to school, specifically to prepare for entrance to Cambridge. In June 1661, undoubtedly with the benefit of the advice and influence of Humphrey Babington, he presented himself at Trinity College, and on 8 July he was formally admitted to the university. At 18, he was older than most new undergraduates; wealthy young gentlemen were often admitted at the tender age of 14, accompanied by a servant to look after them.

Some idea of the enthusiasm with which Newton's mother viewed the enterprise can be gleaned from the fact that, far from having his own servant, he entered the college at the lowest level, as a so-called subsizar, who paid for his keep by acting as a servant himself for the Fellows, and even for wealthy students. Newton's own allowance was £10 a year, from a mother whose income by now was about £700 a year. At its worst, being a subsizar could be extremely unpleasant, and include the duty of emptying the chamber pots of the more affluent students. But apparently Newton did not have to sink that low. Technically he was the servant of Humphrey Babington (who was seldom in residence in Cambridge), and so had few menial duties to perform. Nevertheless, he can hardly have enjoyed this status.

From the information we have, Newton seems to have spent a miserable first year and a half in Cambridge, lost in solitary study and lacking any real friends. Things only improved when, early in 1663, he met Nicholas Wickins. Newton and Wickins were both unhappy with their room-mates, and agreed to room together. The arrangement suited both of them so much that it continued for 20 years (on the basis of the flimsiest evidence, some people have suggested that Newton was a homosexual, either practising or latent; our reaction is, 'so what?'). What little we know of Newton's way of life in those years comes from Wickins, via his son, John. None of Newton's other contemporaries as Cambridge undergraduates left any recollection of him, confirming that he was still a quiet thinker who kept himself to himself.

In fact, being a solitary thinker who loved books was the best way to learn in Cambridge in those days. Only a third of the students who entered left with a degree, even though about the only requirement for graduating was to stay there for four years. Although it had been one of the best universities when it was founded in the thirteenth century, by the second half of the seventeenth century Cambridge was, by European standards, a backwater where Aristotle was still taught by rote, and the only relevant training it gave was for a career in the Church or (barely) medicine. The only scientific professorship, the Lucasian Chair of Mathematics, was established in 1663, and awarded to Isaac Barrow, previously a Professor of Greek. And, more than 30 years after the publication of Galileo's *Dialogue*, the Sun-centred Copernican cosmology was still disapproved of in

Cambridge, in spite of the usual English love of anything the Papacy hated.

Whatever Newton learned, he learned on his own, studying the writings of Galileo and Descartes, among others. He was awarded a scholarship in April 1664, presumably because he was a good student (and very possibly partly due to Babington's influence), and automatically received his BA in January 1665. With the scholarship came the promise of a continued place at Cambridge until 1668, when he would become an MA; during that time, he could study whatever he liked – or, indeed, nothing at all.

Around that time, between receiving the scholarship and graduating, Newton's love of experimentation led him to use himself as a guinea pig in a series of alarming tests. First, he stared at the Sun with one eye for as long as he could bear, in order to study the after-images produced when he looked away. He nearly blinded himself (*never* try this yourself!) and recovered his sight only after being shut up in the dark for several days. Undaunted, a little later he poked a bodkin into his eye, between the ball of the eye and the bone of the socket, and pressed it against his eyeball to observe the way the distortion affected his sight.

It is possible that Newton's interest in mathematics, and through that, science, was stimulated by the first series of lectures given by Barrow as Lucasian Professor, in the spring of 1664. It is certain that he became so absorbed in his studies that, Wickins tells us, he would forget to eat and would stay up all night at his books, becoming while still in his twenties the epitome of the absent-minded professor. He was careless about his dress, and there is no evidence that he ever took a bath – not that that was so unusual in seventeenth-century England.

By the time he graduated, or soon after, Newton was already well on the way to developing calculus, and had (as we have seen!) begun his study of light. Then came one of the most famous episodes in his life.

The plague arrived in Cambridge in 1665, and led to the temporary closure of the university. Some students moved out to nearby villages with their tutors, and tried to carry on a semblance of normal life. But Newton had his BA, and worked alone anyway. So in the summer of 1665 he returned to Lincolnshire, where he stayed until March 1666. The spread of the disease had halted during the winter months, and it seemed safe to return to Cambridge; but when the warm weather came back so did the plague, and in June Newton left for Lincolnshire again, returning to Cambridge permanently in April 1667, when the plague had run its course.

The period in Lincolnshire is often referred to as Newton's *annus mirabilis*, even though it lasted for the best part of two years. Popular accounts also depict him at Woolsthorpe for most of this time, although in fact, as well as the abortive return to Cambridge in 1666, he spent some (perhaps much) of the time at Humphrey Babington's rectory in Boothby Pagnell. No matter – the important point is that, in Newton's own words, written half a century later, 'in those days [1665–6] I was in the prime of my age for invention & minded Mathematicks & Philosophy more than at any time since'. By the end of 1666, he was just 24 years old.

Although the mathematical achievements were breathtaking for a young man working entirely on his own, we shall skip over them; everybody knows that differential calculus is important, but only mathematicians care about how Newton came to invent it. What everybody wants to know about is the story of the apple – whether it is true, and how it provides insight into the universal nature of gravity. The story is at least half-true. There was an apple, but it didn't fall on Newton's head. What Newton puzzled over during the plague years was the tendency of the Moon to recede from the Earth by virtue of its motion in its orbit: the puzzle of what Huygens had recently dubbed the 'centrifugal force'. Why did the Moon stay in its orbit, and not fly off at a tangent?

This is a deeper question than it seems to us now. Only a generation before, Galileo had been the first person to understand inertia, and to realize that a moving object will keep moving unless some force acts to slow it down. But even he thought that the natural tendency of a moving object is to move in circles, which is why planets stay in orbit around the Sun, and the Moon stays in orbit around the Earth. (Galileo was no fool, and came to these conclusions because he reasoned that an object moving 'in a straight line' towards the horizon on Earth is actually moving in a circle around the Earth's circumference.) It had been Descartes who saw that the natural tendency is for a body to keep moving in a straight line unless acted upon by some external force. So Newton's generation was the first (and, as it turned out, only) one for which there was a real puzzle about why the Moon did not fly off into space.

Centrifugal force also comes into the Galileo story in another way. Opponents of the idea that the Earth was rotating (there were still such people even in the 1660s!) sometimes argued that if it were, everything on the surface would be flung off into space by centrifugal force. Of course, such 'philosophers' didn't bother to dirty their hands by carrying out calculations, they just regarded this argument as a triumph of pure reason over the foolishness of Galileo and Copernicus. Newton was different. He calculated the strength of this outward force due to the Earth's rotation, and showed that it is much smaller (nearly 300 times smaller) than the inward tug of gravity, measured at the surface of the Earth.

Then Newton had the idea that the influence of this inward tug might extend outwards into space. This is where the apple comes in. One day, while thinking intently about centrifugal force and gravity (either at Woolsthorpe or at Boothby Pagnell), he saw an apple fall from a tree. If the power of gravity could extend to the top of a tree, he thought, how much higher could it extend? Indeed, why should it be limited at all? Suppose it extended as far as the Moon?

He calculated the centrifugal force trying to fling the Moon out of its orbit by virtue of its motion around the Earth, and discovered that it was almost exactly the same size as the strength the Earth's gravity would have at the distance of the Moon, if the strength of gravity fell off as the inverse of the square of the distance from the centre of the Earth (only 'almost', because at this time he used a slightly incorrect estimate of the radius of the Earth). And using Kepler's laws, which describe mathematically the elliptical orbits of the planets around the Sun, he found that 'the endeavours [of the planets] of receding from the Sun will be reciprocally as the squares of the distances from the Sun.'

In other words, a planet twice as far from the Sun 'endeavours to recede' one-quarter as strongly, a planet three times as far feels one-ninth of the force, and so on. The implication was that if a force proportional to one over the distance squared was trying to fling the planets out of their orbits, and yet they stayed in orbit, there must be an exactly equal and opposite force holding them in place – gravity. But Newton didn't quite spell that out in 1666.

Newton's investigation of colours began in Cambridge before the plague years, and was largely abandoned while he was in Lincolnshire. But once back at Trinity he completed his investigations, using triangular prisms to break up light from the Sun into the rainbow pattern of the spectrum. Earlier investigators, including Robert Hooke, had projected the spectrum on to a screen a metre or so away, seeing a white spot of light with coloured edges. Newton projected his spectrum on to a wall 7 metres from the prism, and saw a spectrum five times as long as it was wide, which could not be explained as a coloured image of the Sun. The received wisdom about colours at that time was that white represented pure light, and that colours were formed by adding in increasing amounts of black to the white. Newton showed that white light is not pure at all, but is made up of a mixture of all the colours of the rainbow (black is simply the absence of light). He went on to develop a new theory of light and colour, based on the idea of light being a stream of tiny particles.

The most astonishing thing about all this – three major breakthroughs, in different areas of science, any one of which would have made his reputation – is that Newton hugged all his results to himself. He seems to have been genuinely uninterested in fame, and to have studied nature simply for his own interest, for the pleasure of finding things out. But the way he hid his light under a bushel for so long is particularly odd because in 1667 he could have done with a little recognition.

That year there was an election of Fellows at Trinity. This was not a common event – there had been no elections for the previous three years – and there were only nine vacancies. Election as a Fellow would give Newton a few more years of security. The first rung on the ladder was a minor Fellowship, which would automatically become a major Fellowship when he became an MA in 1668. He would then have a further seven years to do anything he liked, or nothing at all, which is what most Fellows did, before being required under the statutes to take holy orders. (In the seventeenth century, Cambridge University was still a Church-oriented establishment.)

There is one clue as to why Newton should have succeeded in being elected as a minor Fellow in October 1667, when his work was completely unknown, and most such appointments depended crucially on influence and patronage. Earlier that year, Humphrey Babington had become one of the Senior Fellows of the college. The oath that Newton swore on taking up his Fellowship included the promise that 'I will either set Theology as the object of my studies and will take holy orders when the time prescribed by these statutes arrives, or I will resign from the college.'

Secure for the time being, Newton continued his solitary studies in mathematics and his investigations of light and colour, becoming (if anything) increasingly absent-minded and vague in everyday matters. He had only three friends: John Wickins, Humphrey Babington and Isaac Barrow. We know tantalizingly little about any of these friendships, although clearly Newton must have discussed mathematics with Barrow, who became aware of his ability.

There are many stories of how Newton was often so deep in thought that he would sit down for dinner at high table in the hall and forget to eat anything during the entire course of a meal; how he never took any exercise (begrudging time spent away from his studies); and how, on the rare occasions he had a visitor, he might step into his study for a bottle of wine, forget the purpose of his mission and sit down at his desk to work. But the other Fellows were well aware that they had a rare genius in their midst. When Newton walked in the Fellows' garden and traced diagrams in the gravel with his stick, the other Fellows would carefully avoid treading on the diagrams, which stayed visible for weeks.

Bizarrely to modern eyes, towards the end of the 1660s Newton developed a consuming passion for alchemy. This was to absorb him, on and off for years, in the study of what even then were thought of as disreputable texts and the carrying out of experiments with various noxious substances. But we shall largely ignore these activities since they have no bearing on his stature as the greatest scientist.

About the same time (in 1669), the outside world of science showed the first sign of breaking in on Newton's isolation. The mathematician Nicolaus Mercator (not the cartographer, Gerardus Mercator) published a book which took some of the first steps down the mathematical road Newton had already travelled. John Collins, a government clerk in London who was a kind of maths groupie, sent a copy to Isaac Barrow, who knew enough about Newton's work to realize that his priority was threatened.

Under pressure from Barrow, for the first time Newton suffered the anguish he was to experience whenever he was asked to publish his work. He prepared a paper, going far beyond Mercator but still only hinting at how far he had actually gone, and sent it to Collins. Then he asked for it back, deciding not to publish. But Collins knew enough about maths to recognize a work of genius when he saw one, and made a copy, which he kept and showed around – perhaps a little indiscreetly. Word began to spread that there was a new mathematician of note in Cambridge.

This flurry of activity, abortive though it seems, may have been important in providing Newton with his next step up the academic ladder. In 1669, Barrow decided to resign his chair. His motives are unclear, but seem to have been an unholy mixture of a genuine desire to devote more time to divinity, and an ambition to do better for himself. It is certainly *not* true that he simply decided that Newton was a genius who deserved the job more! There is nothing about the seedy and self-serving atmosphere of Cambridge in those days, nor about the known character of Barrow, to suggest such altruism. Since Barrow soon became a Royal Chaplain and then, in 1673, Master of Trinity College, it was clearly a good career move on his part.

Barrow's influence was amply sufficient to ensure that the man he wanted should replace him as Lucasian Professor, and the man he wanted was Isaac Newton, who he now knew to be the ablest mathematician in Europe. The post was one of the most desirable in Cambridge. It brought with it an income of £100 a year (remember that, as a Fellow, Newton already had free board and lodging, and a little additional income), with no tutoring responsibilities. The sole requirement of the position was to give one course of lectures a year – though even this requirement was often abused. It was a secure tenure for life – and it was Newton's, at the age of 26. There was one peculiarity about the bequest under which Henry Lucas had established the chair: it specifically barred any holder from accepting a position in the Church requiring residence outside Cambridge or 'the cure of souls'. This was to prove a godsend to Newton.

Newton must have imagined that he could now return to a life of quiet anonymity. But his own inventiveness, and Barrow's interest in his work, were soon to thrust him firmly into the spotlight.

Newton's work on optics and colour in the late 1660s led him to think about telescopes. In those days, one of the major problems with existing telescopes, which used lenses – *refracting* telescopes – was that the lenses produced coloured fringes around the image of the object being viewed. From his experiments, Newton knew that there was no way these fringes could be avoided using simple lenses. (In fact, modern telescopes do solve the problem by using compound lenses made from more than one kind of material, but this was way beyond the technology available to Newton.) But also he realized that a *reflecting* telescope, in which the magnifying is done by a curved mirror instead of a lens, would not suffer from this problem.

Characteristically, in order to demonstrate the value of a reflecting telescope, Newton built one. We now know that he wasn't the first – Leonard Digges built one, probably on the same principles as Newton's telescope, before 1550. But Newton knew nothing of this, and produced his design independently.

The problem with a reflector is that in its simplest form the head of the observer would be in the mouth of the telescope, blocking out any incoming light. There had been another design for a reflecting telescope, drawn up by James Gregory in 1663, but this used two curved mirrors, the second a small one in the mouth of the telescope to reflect light from the main mirror back through a hole in the middle of the main mirror. The Gregorian telescope was not built at that time, and only became used in astronomy much later. In Newton's simpler design, a small flat mirror at an angle of 45 degrees in the mouth of the instrument deflects light sideways, where the observer can view comfortably without interfering with the operation of the instrument. And Newton actually built his instrument, using a metal mirror he shaped and polished himself.

In fact, he may have built two, one around 1667 or 1668, which no more is heard of, and one in 1671 (possibly, it was one telescope that he put aside for a couple of years and then got out again). It was about 15 centimetres long, and allegedly enlarged as well as a refractor 3 metres long. Late in life, Newton was asked where he got it made, and replied that he had made it himself. His questioner then asked where he got the tools, and he laughed and said that he made them as well, for 'if I had staid for other people to make my tools & things for me, I had never made anything of it'.

Collins learned about the telescope before the end of the 1660s, and word spread both from him and from visitors to Cambridge who had seen the instrument. The newly formed Royal Society heard of it before the end of 1671, and asked for a demonstration of its powers. It was Isaac Barrow who took the telescope to London and showed it to them. It caused a sensation. Newton was immediately elected as a Fellow of the Royal Society (the formal ceremony took place on 11 January 1672), and became famous in scientific circles, first in England and almost immediately in Europe, as the Society spread the news of this great English invention.

Ironically, it never proved possible in Newton's time to make a reflector big enough, and with an accurate enough mirror, for serious astronomical work. The immediate effect of his sudden acceptance as a leading scientist was that he felt secure enough to send his theory of light and colours to the Royal Society for publication. This led to a bitter row with Robert Hooke, the first 'curator of experiments' at the Society, and one of its leading lights. He complained both that Newton's ideas were rubbish, and that what was any good in the theory had already been thought of by himself. (This was typical of Hooke, who scattered vague ideas around like buckshot, and whenever someone else came up with a complete theory of anything, he said he had done it first.) The row simmered until 1675, and led to Newton's famous remark that 'if I have seen further it is by standing on the shoulders of Giants'.

This was not, as many people surmise, a reference to his work on gravity, which was not public knowledge then. Instead, the remark was made in a letter to Hooke in 1675, intended to close the correspondence on light – a letter couched in superficially polite terms, but with a vicious subtext. John Faulkner, of the Lick Observatory, has argued persuasively that, among other things, the reference to 'Giants' with a capital 'G' was a deliberately offensive reference to the fact that Hooke was physically a very short man, intended to imply that he was also an intellectual pygmy.

Whatever, Newton was furious that anybody should doubt his word and belittle his ideas, and equally angry at the time he had to waste defending his theory of light, when he could be doing new work. He threatened to resign from the Royal Society, and when persuaded to stay he instructed the Secretary, Henry Oldenburg, not to forward any correspondence to him because 'I intend to be no further solicitous about matters of Philosophy'. He withdrew once again into his shell in Cambridge, where he had already started a new line of study that almost immediately led to a personal crisis which threatened the bedrock of his life – his hold on the Lucasian chair. Against that background, his row with Hooke (who remained a lifelong enemy) and his decision to sever his connections with the Royal Society (if not his membership) take on a different complexion.

In about 1672, just after he became a Fellow of the Royal Society, Newton began a serious study of theology, alongside his alchemical experiments. By then, he was more than half-way through the initial seven-year period of his major Fellowship, and coming up to the time when he would have to take holy orders. To most Cambridge Fellows, this was a ritual that caused them no second thoughts. But Newton never did anything by halves, and started preparing himself for the event. Typically, once started down a new avenue of investigation he delved obsessively deeper and deeper into his studies. Before long, he had convinced himself that the whole foundation of established religion in England was based on a corruption of the original biblical texts, and specifically that the concept of the Holy Trinity, placing Jesus Christ on an equal footing with God, was a false one.

This idea was known as Arianism, after Arius, who founded the doctrine and was excommunicated in 321 for his beliefs. It was incompatible with the teaching of the established Church in England – and deliciously inappropriate for a Fellow of the Cambridge college named in honour of the Holy Trinity. In taking holy orders, Newton would have to state on oath his belief in the Holy Trinity, and this he was not now prepared to do. To him, worshipping Christ as God would be idolatry, a mortal sin that would put his soul in peril. But without ordination, there would be no continuing membership of Cambridge University, and therefore no Lucasian chair. It would be back to the farm in Lincolnshire.

As 1675 approached, all of this was vastly more important to Newton than any quibbles about optics or mathematics. His more and more detailed researches into theology would continue obsessively for many years, but, like the alchemy, they have no real place in our story except to help explain why he was so secretive in general. By the beginning of 1675, the situation looked so desperate that Newton wrote to Oldenburg requesting to be excused from paying his subscription to the Royal Society, because 'I am to part with my Fellowship, & as my incomes contract, I find it will be convenient that I contract my expenses.'

But he had one last throw of the dice. Isaac Barrow was by now Master of Trinity, and without explaining his true reasons for the request, Newton obtained Barrow's permission to petition the King for a dispensation – not for himself alone as a special case, but for *all* Lucasian Professors, from the requirement of ordination. His argument was that even ordination would be against the spirit of the Lucas bequest, with its specific requirement that a holder of the post should not be active in the Church. The King (still Charles II) had the power to dispense with any statute of the university, for any reason he liked (or for no reason at all). He was interested in science, as patron of the Royal Society, and granted the dispensation in perpetuity, 'to give all just encouragement to learned men who are & shall be elected to the said Professorship'.

Newton was safe. After this crisis, plus the unpleasantness with Hooke, it is small wonder that he laid low in Cambridge, deep in his theological and alchemical studies, and generally let the world of science get on with things in its own way. No doubt he felt his decision reinforced when Oldenburg died and Hooke was elected as his successor as Secretary of the Royal Society in 1677. If you think Newton was being obsessively cautious in going to such lengths to conceal his Arianism, it's worth noting that his eventual successor as Lucasian Professor, William Whiston, was dismissed from his post in 1710 for publicly discussing what he saw to be errors in the Anglican faith.

Newton rarely left Cambridge in the years that followed, the notable exception being in 1679, when his mother became ill, and he went to be with her in Woolsthorpe while she died. As both her heir and executor, he had to spend several months putting the affairs of the estate in order. But although he did not visit other scientists, he did allow himself to be drawn into some correspondence, including another encounter with Hooke. This time, the discussion concerned the hypothetical trajectory that would be followed by an object falling from the surface of the rotating Earth towards the centre of the Earth, if it could move through the solid Earth without resistance. During the correspondence, Hooke suggested that the object would move around the centre of the Earth in an ellipse (which was wrong), and also made a garbled reference to an inverse-square law.

The outside world of science also intruded on Newton during the winter of 1680–81, when a new comet was seen on two occasions. The Astronomer Royal, John Flamsteed, realized that what had been seen was one comet first approaching the Sun, being lost in the Sun's glare, and then retreating from the Sun. Previously, it had been thought that such appearances were of two separate comets. But Flamsteed imagined some kind of magnetic repulsion, in which the comet was turned around before reaching the Sun. Newton reasoned that the comet must have gone round the far side of the Sun in a curving path more like an elongated planetary orbit. Almost in spite of himself, Newton's attention had been drawn back to thinking about gravity and orbits. The interest was fanned further by the appearance of another comet (now called Halley's Comet) in 1682.

Then came another disturbance in his private life. Newton's long-time friend, roommate and scribe John Wickins decided to resign his Fellowship in 1683. He left Cambridge to become Rector of Stoke Edith, in Herefordshire, and married. The limited correspondence between the two suggests some bitterness about the break-up of the old friendship, at least on Newton's side. On the practical side, Wickins was quickly replaced by a young man from Newton's old school in Grantham, his namesake Humphrey Newton. Neither Humphrey nor Isaac claimed that they were related, but there may have been a distant connection. Humphrey stayed with Newton for five years as a kind of amanuensis, copying out his works and probably acting partly as a servant; it is from him that some of the more colourful accounts of Newton's life in Cambridge have come. Among other things, it was Humphrey Newton who made the fair copy of Isaac Newton's greatest work, the copy from which the book *Principia* was printed.

The story of how Newton came to write his masterpiece is well known. At a meeting of the Royal Society in January 1684, Edmond Halley, Christopher Wren and Robert Hooke had a discussion about planetary orbits. They had come to see that the orbits of the planets around the Sun, in accordance with Kepler's Laws, obeyed an inverse-square law (in fact, Wren had discussed this with Newton in 1677), but they could not prove that an inverse-square law of gravity *must* produce elliptical orbits. For all they knew, it could just be a coincidence. Perhaps one day a new planet would be discovered in a different kind of orbit (indeed, comets seemed at that time to have different kinds of orbit). Hooke, typically, infuriated his colleagues by claiming to have a proof that an inverse-square law strictly required elliptical orbits, but he wasn't going to tell them what it was.

What happened over the next few months we do not know, but it seems very likely that Halley was stung into further action by his irritation with Hooke. In August, he went to Cambridge to see the man regarded as the best mathematician in Europe (even if he had been keeping quiet lately), and the one who could surely be relied on to find a way to put Hooke in his place.

After some preliminary chit-chat, Halley asked Newton if he knew what curve would be followed by a planet attracted to the Sun by an inverse-square law. Newton immediately said that it would be an ellipse. Asked how he knew, Newton replied that he had done the calculation some time ago. When Halley pressed him, Newton claimed to have lost the relevant piece of paper, but promised to send it down to Halley in London when he had time to find it.

Of course, the paper was not lost. Newton was playing for time – reluctant, as ever, to let the world know of his discoveries, and endure the time-wasting public attention that would result. But this time, perhaps motivated by the still burning desire to put one over on Hooke, he succumbed. When he did dig out his calculations, he found a small error, and sat down to work them out again. As always, once he became embroiled in a problem he could not stop. In November 1684, Halley received a nine-page paper not only proving the relationship of the inverse-square law of gravity to planetary orbits, but hinting that this was just the tip of the iceberg of a larger body of work.

The paper, 'On the motion of bodies in an orbit', was a dramatic step forward. Halley presented it to the Royal Society on 10 December. Encouraged by Halley (with the enthusiastic support of the Society), and gripped again by his desire to get everything sorted out in his own mind, Newton abandoned everything else – even his alchemy – and threw himself into writing what became his great book, *Philosophiae Naturalis Principia Mathematica*. Halley nursemaided the whole enterprise, cajoling Newton when he became reluctant to finish the work, and soothing him when, inevitably, Hooke claimed that he had done it all years before. (As a result, Newton went through the manuscript at a late stage, savagely removing all references to Hooke; there is no doubt that Hooke was lying, since when Halley told him to produce evidence that he had done the work first, or shut up, he shut up.) Halley read the proofs of the book, and even paid for its publication when the Royal Society, in desperate financial straits, found that it had insufficient funds for the task; happily, Halley actually made a small profit on the deal. The great work was eventually published in July

1687, completing the scientific revolution that had been begun by Galileo.

As well as his law of gravitation (his *universal* law of gravitation), Newton provided in the book the three laws of motion which formed the foundation on which physics could be built. The first law states that every object continues to be at rest, or to move in a straight line at a constant speed, unless it is acted upon by an external force. The second law states that the acceleration of an object (the rate at which its velocity changes, which means either its speed, or the direction it is moving in, or both) is proportional to the force acting on it. And the third law states that whenever a force is applied to an object, it responds with an equal and opposite force – if you press your finger against the wall, the wall resists your push.

There is another fundamental piece of physics in the *Principia* which is not always given the attention it deserves. The gravitational force considered by Newton was an action at a distance. He did not require the existence of any medium between the Sun and the planets to transmit the force of gravity – it was not as if the planets were tied to the

Sun by elastic, or held in place by mysterious swirling vortices of some invisible fluid (an idea seriously put forward by Descartes). This was a dramatic and revolutionary suggestion at the time, but became deeply embedded as part of physics – so deeply, that modern readers don't think it odd at all.

Without doubt, Newton had well and truly arrived. He was hailed as a genius, and could never again retreat into isolation. But he had also, in his 45th year, virtually stopped being a scientist. When nobody had heard of him, he was the greatest scientist that ever lived; when he was hailed as such, he stopped being a scientist. Even the *Principia*, great though it was, was a masterly summation of ideas developed up to 20 years before. From now on, Isaac Newton would be a public figure, but although he would continue to impress the world with his scientific publications, they would almost all be old material that he had kept to himself for years, waiting until the time was ripe for publication.

Even before writing the *Principia*, Newton had begun to be more active in college life at Trinity, as one of the more senior Fellows. By March 1687 the masterwork was largely off his hands, some already with the printers, one volume being diligently copied out by Humphrey. And Newton had time to make his name in Cambridge in another way, as a principal defender of the rights of the university against the new Catholic King, James II, who had succeeded his brother in 1685.

There was a strong anti-Catholic feeling in England, but by 1687 James had been on the throne for long enough to begin to feel confident, and he tried to throw his weight around. On 9 February, the University of Cambridge was ordered by the King to admit a Benedictine monk, Alban Francis, to the degree of Master of Arts, without requiring him to take any examinations or to swear any oaths. It was quite the done thing to confer degrees in this way (equivalent to a modern honorary degree) on someone like a foreign dignitary, and this had been done before even for Catholics. But the university was well aware that Francis intended to exercise his rights as an MA to participate in the activities of the university. One Benedictine would pose no problem, but surely there would soon be others, voting the Catholic way in the university's affairs.

Although the Cambridge academics feared the prospect, they were largely a bunch of feeble time-servers who lacked the guts to stand up to the King. Astonishingly, in view of the way he had previously avoided any kind of publicity or fuss (but perhaps understandably in view of his Arian beliefs), Newton became one of the most outspoken opponents of the proposal, and was largely instrumental in making the university refuse to accept Francis or award him an MA. This really did take some courage – as a ringleader in the opposition to the King, Newton was among nine Cambridge Fellows who had to appear before the notorious Lord Chancellor, Judge Jeffreys, who in the 'bloody assize' had had 300 people hanged for rebellion the previous year. Remember that this was before the publication of the *Principia*, when Newton was still largely unknown outside academic circles, and had no widespread fame to protect him from the potential consequences of Jeffreys' wrath.

Newton achieved great eminence in Cambridge for this stand. King James was removed at the end of 1688 and replaced by the Protestant William of Orange (grandson of Charles I) and his wife Mary (daughter of James II) in 1689 – the 'Glorious Revolution'. Newton was one of two representatives from the University of Cambridge elected to the Convention Parliament, which legalized the position of William and Mary, and re-established the Anglican Church. The Parliament was dissolved after a year and a month; Newton had played no active part, but kept his mouth shut and voted according to the party line. He did, though, suffer one great disappointment.

One of the Acts passed by the Parliament had increased the legal tolerance shown to religious dissenters. Newton must have hoped that this would enable him to come out as an Arian. But the Act specifically excluded two classes of people from toleration: Catholics, and 'any person that shall deny in his Preaching or Writing the Doctrine of the Blessed Trinity.'

Hiding his disappointment, Newton returned to Cambridge and did not offer himself for re-election to the next parliament. But while in London he had renewed and cultivated an old friendship with Charles Montague, grandson of the Earl of Manchester, struck up when Montague had been a student at Cambridge (indeed, at Trinity, which he entered in 1679). Montague became a powerful political influence during the reign of William and Mary, and this soon totally changed Newton's life.

Not that it wasn't already going through changes. Also in 1689, Newton became firm friends with a young Swiss mathematician, Nicholas Fatio de Duillier (usually referred to as Fatio). He became something of a confidant of Newton's, and passed on news about Newton and his work to a wider audience, including Christiaan Huygens. The friendship remained very close for three years, and led to Fatio being asked to live with Newton in Cambridge and work with him on a second, bigger and better edition of the *Principia*. But nothing came of the suggestion, and by 1693 the relationship was petering out.

About the same time that Newton got to know Fatio, he also met, and struck up a lasting friendship with, the philosopher John Locke. This friendship was cemented by their common anti-Trinitarian views, and a shared interest in alchemy. Another friend, whom

Newton had already met through the Royal Society, was, of course, Samuel Pepys.

With his horizons broadened by his experiences while serving as a Member of Parliament in London, and by friends such as these, Newton found the return to Cambridge life in the early 1690s frustrating. He threw himself into his alchemy, and also began gathering up the threads of all his more public work into a planned great volume summing up his contributions to science. But he also began sounding out opportunities to leave the university altogether and find some other employment. By 1693, his disappointment at failing to find such a post, plus years of overwork and the strain of keeping his Arianism concealed, told at last, and he suffered a major nervous breakdown. It cannot have helped that by then the tedious dispute with Wilhelm Leibniz about who had discovered calculus first was rumbling along; this row is of no interest today, except for the way it may have disturbed Newton's peace of mind.

Few details of the illness survive, except for two bizarre letters, one to Locke and one to Pepys, apologizing for making wild accusations that his friends were conspiring against him, and trying to get him embroiled with women (Locke and Pepys were both known to enjoy female companionship). There have been suggestions that the mental illness was caused by Newton's close proximity for many years to noxious substances during his alchemical experiments. This is unlikely, because he soon made what seems to have been a complete recovery, which doesn't happen with, say, mercury poisoning.

There is also some evidence that Newton had suffered similar, but lesser (or better concealed?) bouts of disturbance before, notably in the months just after Wickins left Cambridge. This parallels the way his depression in 1693 followed the break-up of the friendship with Fatio.

Whatever the causes of the illness, Newton's friends stood by him and helped his recovery. In 1694, he took up an old interest in the problems of the exact orbit of the Moon around the Earth. Since the Moon is influenced by the gravity of the Sun as well as the Earth, this is an example of the 'three body problem' in gravitation, which, it is now known, cannot be solved precisely. It is no wonder that Newton said his head 'never ached but with his studies on the moon'. But by the standards of his great days, this was mere tinkering around the edges of gravitational theory.

It must have come as an immense relief when in 1696 Charles Montague, now Chancellor of the Exchequer and well aware of Newton's desire to leave Cambridge, offered him the post of Warden of the Royal Mint. He accepted with alacrity – the appointment was confirmed on 19 March, and before the end of April Newton had moved to London, lock, stock and barrel. For the rest of his life he never returned to Cambridge, except for a few days, although – having now learned what was expected of a Cambridge Fellow – he retained all his Cambridge posts and the income from them until 1701.

Montague's letter informing Newton of his appointment mentioned that the post was 'worth five or six hundred pounds [a year], and has not too much bus'nesse to require more attendance than you may spare'. It was, in other words, potentially a sinecure. But Newton was never one to shirk a job (except farming), and threw himself into his work. The Warden was actually number two at the

Mint, which was technically run by the Master; but the Master, Thomas Neale, was quite happy to leave all the work to Newton. And work there was. Because of forgery and clipping of silver coins, the currency was debased and there was a serious monetary crisis. Parliament had just passed an Act authorizing a complete recoinage, and it fell to Newton to see this task through. He improved the efficiency of the Mint, cleaned out corruption and completed the task by the summer of 1698. Montague told anyone who would listen that the job would never have been completed had it not been for Newton.

One of Newton's less palatable duties was to prosecute counterfeiters – and a successful prosecution usually meant a hanging. At first, he tried to get out of what he called a 'vexatious & dangerous' task, but when ordered by the Treasury to get on with it, he did so with his customary efficiency and a certain cold-blooded ruthlessness, slightly chilling to us now but quite normal for someone in his position in the 1690s.

At the end of 1699 Thomas Neale died, and even though Montague was no longer in power Newton was quickly appointed as his successor – a recognition of how well he had carried out his work, but a unique promotion in the long history of the Royal Mint. He held the post until he died, although in his later years the real work was deputed to his eventual successor. The appointment was confirmed on 3 February 1700, and the following year Newton finally resigned from his Cambridge posts. He had made £3,500 that year from his post at the Mint, on a complicated profit-sharing basis which was all completely legal and above board (although this was an unusually good year).

With everything running smoothly at the Mint and the recoinage long since completed, in the 1700s Newton became active in other areas. Probably at the behest of Lord Halifax (as Charles Montague had now become), he stood for parliament again in 1701, and was again elected to represent Cambridge, although once again his activity in parliament was limited to voting as he was told to vote. In May 1702 William III died, and parliament was dissolved. Mary had died in 1694, and William was succeeded by Queen Anne, the second daughter of James II. Anne was heavily influenced by Halifax, and it was during the election campaign of 1705 that she knighted both Newton and Halifax's brother.

It didn't help. The political tide was against Halifax and his party; Newton was not elected, and never stood for parliament again. But it is worth recounting the story, since many people believe that Newton was knighted for his scientific achievements, some think that it was a reward for his work at the Mint, and few appreciate that it was a sordid party political ploy that didn't even achieve its intended aim. Newton was, though, the first scientist to be honoured in this way, if 'honoured' is the right word.

By 1705 he was probably happy to be out of politics, since he had recently been elected to the post in which he would, though now in his sixties, make his last, and by no means least, mark on science – President of the Royal Society. The way had been cleared by the death of Newton's old adversary Robert Hooke, in March 1703 at the age of 67. With the opposition out of the way, Newton was elected President on 30 November that year, and his second great book, *Opticks*, was published in 1704. The book had been completed in the mid-1690s, and Newton had quietly waited to publish it until Hooke had died and could not claim to have done it all before.

If anything, the *Opticks* was more successful than the *Principia*, because it was written in easily intelligible language and dealt with ideas, such as light and colour, that everyone could relate to. It was the crowning glory of Newton's scientific reputation, and helped to establish him as not just the most famous but also the most powerful scientist in the land.

He ruled the Royal Society with a rod of iron for more than 20 years, and was by no means universally popular with its members, although he always got a healthy majority of the votes for the presidency. He made the Society truly scientific, attended almost all the meetings until old age and infirmity prevented him, and turned a somewhat dilettantish gentlemen's talking-shop into a truly learned society. He also carried on an unedifying row with John Flamsteed, who had been commissioned by the King to produce a star catalogue, and was being tediously slow (in the view of everyone except Flamsteed and his wife) in producing the goods. But Newton wouldn't have been Newton if he hadn't been rowing with somebody; the Leibniz business also continued to drag on.

But there is a much more interesting insight into Newton's world in London in the early years of the eighteenth century. He had always been generous in providing financial help for his family of half-siblings and their children, and one of those children, his niece Catherine, came to London to be his house-keeper (in the grand sense of running the house; not doing the cooking and dusting, which were jobs for servants).

Catherine was the daughter of Newton's half-sister Hannah Smith, who had married a Robert Barton. She was born in 1679, and her father died in 1693, leaving her family destitute. Newton settled all their financial troubles, and in the mid-1690s, when she was about 17, Catherine Barton came to look after his house (then in Jermyn Street, later in St Martin's Street, just south of present-day Leicester Square).

Catherine was a strikingly good-looking, charming young woman who was a great asset to Newton, and she naturally came to know all his circle of friends, including Lord Halifax (who was some 20 years younger than Newton). In 1706, when he drew up his will, Halifax added a codicil in which he left £3,000 and all his jewels to Catherine, 'as a small Token of the great Love and Affection I have long had for her'. In October 1706, Halifax purchased an annuity for Catherine, providing her with £200 a year for the rest of her life. And in February 1713, he replaced the codicil in her favour by one giving her £5,000 and the Lodge of Bushey Park to use in her lifetime 'as a Token of the sincere Love, Affection, and Esteem I have long had for her Person, and as a small Recompence for the Pleasure and Happiness I have had in her Conversation'.

To put the bequest in perspective, Halifax's total estate was worth £150,000 when he died in 1715, and Newton received a bequest of £100. Flamsteed, by now Newton's bitter enemy, took great delight, when the will was made public, in writing to a friend that Newton's niece had been well rewarded 'for her *excellent conversation*' (his emphasis). Catherine received the financial part of the bequest, but not the use of the Lodge, which actually belonged to the Crown. Two years later, she married John Conduitt; he was 29, and she was 38. After about 1725, Conduitt largely took over Newton's work at the Mint, and on Newton's death he managed to secure the Mastership formally for himself. It was through the Conduitts, and their daughter (also named Catherine) that Newton's papers were preserved largely intact, and eventually found a home in the library at the University of Cambridge.

Having plucked his favourite niece from the prospect of poverty in the provinces, and having been a farmer's boy himself, Newton would surely have been delighted had he lived to see his grand-niece Catherine, helped in no small measure by the leg up the social ladder that he had given her mother, marry the Honorable John Wallop, Viscount Lymington, in 1740 – and to see their son, his great-grandnephew, become the second Earl of Portsmouth.

In his declining years, Newton's circle of friends included Prince George (later George II) and his wife Caroline, whom he visited regularly (Queen Anne had been succeeded by the absentee King George in 1714, who was succeeded by George II in 1727). Newton was rich – when he died, his estate was worth more than £30,000 – famous and successful, and he was known as a generous benefactor of his extended family and of charity. His books had been reprinted in various editions, and his place in posterity was assured. But, like all of us, he was in the end a mere mortal. In 1725 illness obliged him to move out of London to the village of Kensington, where the air proved better for him and the Conduitts looked after him with loving care.

But on Christmas Day that year he was 83 years old, and the improvement could not last long. He died on 20 March 1727, in severe pain from a stone in the bladder. At the very last, knowing that death was imminent, he refused the sacrament of the Church, the only public acknowledgement he ever made of his Arianism (at least, semi-public; the only witnesses were John and Catherine Conduitt, and the priest).

Sir Isaac Newton was buried in Westminster Abbey, on 28 March 1727. The best description of the occasion was provided by Voltaire, who saw it and said that it was like 'the funeral of a King who had done well by his subjects'.

Afterword

There is no need for us to try to sum up the impact of Newton's work on science after his death. The greatest scientist of the first half of the twentieth century, the man who has become the very symbol of science in modern times, has made Newton's pre-eminence clear in tones which brook no argument. In a foreword to a twentieth-century edition of Newton's *Opticks*, Albert Einstein wrote:

> Nature was to him an open book, whose letters he could read without effort. The conceptions which he used to reduce the material of experience to order seemed to flow spontaneously from experience itself, from the beautiful experiments which he ranged in order like playthings and describes with an affectionate wealth of detail. In one person, he combined the experimenter, the theorist, the mechanic and, not least, the artist in exposition. He stands before us strong, certain, and alone; his joy in creation and his minute precision are evident in every word and every figure.

A brief history of science

All science is either physics or stamp collecting.

Ernest Rutherford

c. 2000 BC	First phase of construction at Stonehenge, an early observatory.
430 BC	Democritus teaches that everything is made of atoms.
c. 330 BC	Aristotle teaches that the Universe is made of concentric spheres, centred on the Earth.
300 BC	Euclid gathers together and writes down the mathematical knowledge of his time.
265 BC	Archimedes discovers his principle of buoyancy while having a bath.
c. 235 BC	Eratosthenes of Cyrene calculates the size of the Earth with commendable accuracy.

AD 79	Pliny the Elder dies while studying an eruption of Mount Vesuvius.
400	The term 'chemistry' is used for the first time, by scholars in Alexandria.
c. 1020	Alhazen, the greatest scientist of the so-called Dark Ages, explains the workings of lenses and parabolic mirrors.
1054	Chinese astronomers observe a supernova; the remnant is visible today as the Crab Nebula.
1490	Leonardo da Vinci studies the capillary action of liquids.
1543	In his book *De revolutionibus*, Nicholas Copernicus places the Sun, not the Earth, at the centre of the Solar System. Andreas Vesalius studies human anatomy in a scientific way.
c. 1550	The reflecting telescope, and

later the refracting telescope, pioneered by Leonard Digges.

1572	Tycho Brahe observes a supernova.
1580	Prospero Alpini realizes that plants come in two sexes.
1596	Botanical knowledge is summarized in John Gerrard's *Herbal*.
1608	Hans Lippershey's invention of a refracting telescope is the first for which there is firm evidence.
1609–19	Johannes Kepler publishes his laws of planetary motion.
1610	Galileo Galilei observes the moons of Jupiter through a telescope.
1628	William Harvey publishes his discovery of the circulation of the blood.
1643	Mercury barometer invented by Evangelista Torricelli.
1656	Christiaan Huygens correctly

identifies the rings of Saturn, and invents the pendulum clock.

1662   The law relating the pressure and volume of a gas discovered by Robert Boyle, and named after him.

1665   Robert Hooke describes living cells.

1668   A functional reflecting telescope is made by Isaac Newton, unaware of Digges's earlier work.

1673   Antony van Leeuwenhoeck reports his discoveries with the microscope to the Royal Society.

1675   Ole Roemer measures the speed of light by timing eclipses of the moons of Jupiter.

1683   Van Leeuwenhoeck observes bacteria.

1687   Publication of Newton's

Principia, which includes his law of gravitation.

1705   Edmond Halley publishes his prediction of the return of the comet that now bears his name.

1737   Carl Linnaeus publishes his classification of plants.

1749   Georges Louis Leclerc, Comte de Buffon, defines a species in the modern sense.

1758   Halley's Comet returns, as predicted.

1760   John Michell explains earthquakes.

1772   Carl Scheele discovers oxygen; Joseph Priestley independently discovers it two years later.

1773   Pierre de Laplace begins his work on refining planetary orbits. When asked by Napoleon why there was no mention of God in his scheme, Laplace replied, 'I have no need of that hypothesis.'

1783 John Michell is the first person to suggest the existence of 'dark stars' – now known as black holes.

1789 Antoine Lavoisier publishes a table of thirty-one chemical elements.

1796 Edward Jenner carries out the first inoculation, against smallpox.

1798 Henry Cavendish determines the mass of the Earth.

1802 Thomas Young publishes his first paper on the wave theory of light.
Jean-Baptiste Lamarck invents the term 'biology'.

1803 John Dalton proposes the atomic theory of matter.

1807 Humphry Davy discovers sodium and potassium, and

goes on to find several other elements.

1811   Amedeo Avogadro proposes the law that gases contain equal numbers of molecules under the same conditions.

1816   Augustin Fresnel develops his version of the wave theory of light.

1826   First photograph from nature obtained by Nicéphore Niépce.

1828   Friedrich Wöhler synthesizes an organic compound (urea) from inorganic ingredients.

1830   Publication of the first volume of Charles Lyell's *Principles of Geology*.

1831   Michael Faraday and Joseph Henry discover electromagnetic induction. Charles Darwin sets sail on the *Beagle*.

1837   Louis Agassiz coins the term

'ice age' (*die Eiszeit*).

1842	Christian Doppler describes the effect that now bears his name.
1849	Hippolyte Fizeau measures the speed of light to within 5 per cent of the modern value.
1851	Jean Foucault uses his eponymous pendulum to demonstrate the rotation of the Earth.
1857	Publication of Darwin's *Origin of Species*. Coincidentally, Gregor Mendel begins his experiments with pea breeding.
1864	James Clerk Maxwell formulates equations describing all electric and magnetic phenomena, and shows that light is an electromagnetic wave.
1868	Jules Janssen and Norman

Lockyer identify helium from its lines in the Sun's spectrum.

1871   Dmitri Mendeleyev predicts that 'new' elements will be found to fit the gaps in his periodic table.

1887   Experiment carried out by Albert Michelson and Edward Morley finds no evidence for the existence of an 'aether'.

1895   X-rays discovered by Wilhelm Röntgen. Sigmund Freud begins to develop psychoanalysis.

1896   Antoine Becquerel discovers radioactivity.

1897   Electron identified by J. J. Thomson.

1898   Marie and Pierre Curie discover radium.

1900   Max Planck explains how electromagnetic radiation is absorbed and emitted as quanta. Various biologists rediscover Medel's principles of genetics and heredity.

| 1903 | First powered and controlled flight in an aircraft heavier than air, by Orville Wright. |

1905   Einstein's special theory of relativity published.

1908   Hermann Minkowski shows that the special theory of relativity can be elegantly explained in geometrical terms if time is the fourth dimension.

1909   First use of the word 'gene', by Wilhelm Johannsen.

1912   Discovery of cosmic rays by Victor Hess. Alfred Wegener proposes the idea of continental drift, which led in the 1960s to the theory of plate tectonics.

1913   Discovery of the ozone layer by Charles Fabry.

1914	Ernest Rutherford discovers the proton, a name he coins in 1919.
1915	Einstein presents his general theory of relativity to the Prussian Academy of Sciences.
1916	Karl Schwarzschild shows that the general theory of relativity predicts the existence of what are now called black holes.
1919	Arthur Eddington and others observe the bending of starlight during a total eclipse of the Sun, and so confirm the accuracy of the general theory of relativity. Rutherford splits the atom.
1923	Louis de Broglie suggests that electrons can behave as waves.
1926	Enrico Fermi and Paul Dirac discover the statistical rules which govern the behaviour

of quantum particles such as electrons.

1927	Werner Heisenberg develops the uncertainty principle.
1928	Alexander Fleming discovers penicillin.
1929	Edwin Hubble discovers that the Universe is expanding.
1930s	Linus Pauling explains chemistry in terms of quantum physics.
1932	Neutron discovered by James Chadwick.
1937	Grote Reber builds the first radio telescope.
1942	First controlled nuclear reaction achieved by Enrico Fermi and others.
1940s	George Gamow, Ralph Alpher and Robert Herman develop the Big Bang theory of the origin of the Universe.
1948	Richard Feynman extends quantum theory by

developing quantum electrodynamics.

1951   Francis Crick and James Watson work out the helix structure of DNA, using X-ray results obtained by Rosalind Franklin.

1957   Fred Hoyle, together with William Fowler and Geoffrey and Margaret Burbidge, explains how elements are synthesized inside stars. The laser is devised by Gordon Gould. Launch of first artificial satellite, *Sputnik 1*.

1960   Jacques Monod and Francis Jacob identify messenger RNA.

1961   First part of the genetic code cracked by Marshall Nirenberg.

1963   Discovery of quasars by Maarten Schmidt.

1964	W.D. Hamilton explains altruism in terms of what is now called sociobiology.
1965	Arno Penzias and Robert Wilson discover the cosmic background radiation left over from the Big Bang.
1967	Discovery of the first pulsar by Jocelyn Bell.
1979	Alan Guth starts to develop the inflationary model of the very early Universe.
1988	Scientists at Caltech discover that there is nothing in the laws of physics that forbids time travel.
1995	Top quark identified.
1996	Tentative identification of evidence of primitive life in a meteorite believed to have originated on Mars.